I0620795

Dedication

This is book is dedicated to my beloved children, nieces and nephews and to all the parents and young dreamers. May this book bring you joy, love and blessings.

This book belongs to

Ramadaan is the 9th month of the Islamic calendar.
Just like September is the 9th month of the calendar.
Ramdaan comes once a year and each year it starts
on a different day due to the moon.
The moon is then spotted by special people that are
experienced in moon sighting.
Once this is confirmed, we then know at night time if
we will start fasting the following day.

The moon cycle

Ramadaan day 1

We know when Ramadaan starts by looking for the moon in the sky. When it is this shape, we call it a crescent moon and we then know it is the start of the month Ramadaan.

We all get excited when Ramadaan starts, and our parents start decorating our home.

Do you get excited when the house is decorated?

What does fasting mean?

Fasting means that our grown-ups don't eat or drink from sunrise until sunset.
The meal that we take early morning is our breakfast and it has a special name, called "Suhuur."

The Prophet (peace be upon him) teaches us to have suhuur and said: "Take suhuur as there is a blessing in it."

[Sahih Al-bukhari]

When it is sunset, we can break our fast after fasting the whole day. We call this meal "Iftaar" which is like having our dinner.
The first thing we usually have is dates and water.

Have you ever tried dates?
They are sweet, healthy and delicious!

Do you know where dates come from? Dates grow on a special tree called a palm tree, which are usually found in Arabic countries. Let's have a look at what these look like.

After breaking our fast we get ready to pray our
Maghrib prayer.
Sometimes we pray all together at home, and
sometimes our dad and brothers might go to the
Masjid to pray.

After praying, eating and tidying up we usually get ready to go to the Masjid to pray a special prayer. The reason it is special is because we only pray it in the month of Ramadaan. This prayer is called the "Taraweeh" prayer.

In this special month Muslims around the whole world try to become closer to Allah by performing extra good deeds.
Let's find out together what type of things we can do.
Cleaning up after ourselves is a good deed because this helps ourselves and our parents.
This shows care for our belongings, our toys, our pets and plants.

Watering our plants

Looking after our pets

Tidying our toys

Allah loves cleanliness , so cleaning up and helping in the house is a good deed for sure!

Removing something out the way is a good deed too, it could be something as simple as putting rubbish in the bin. You might find a twig on a path and move that out the way so that nobody trips over it.

Helping to clean up

Folding clothes

Putting rubbish in the bin

In Ramadaan we try to remember Allah even more than we normally do. We can do this by performing our salah on time and even add extra prayers.
We can also do this by reading or learning the Quran.
Did you know for every letter that we read in the Quran we get 10 rewards? That is 10 for just one letter!

Another way to become closer to Allah is to give in charity.
When we give to charity in Ramadan our rewards are doubled up! How cool is that?
That's like earning a bonus.
Charity can be in many forms. It can be giving things away; it can be giving money to those in need which is called (zakat) in Arabic.
Just smiling at someone is also considered a charity or helping someone.

So charity comes in many forms.

Giving money to those in need

Giving food to those in need

Giving to young and old

When we fast, we don't only fast by leaving food and drink.

Fasting also means we are careful with what we say.

We must ensure we only use kind words and avoid bad words.

Not to look at bad things or listen to bad things.

Always think about the words you use, are they kind?

Are they good words to use?

Remember Allah loves kindness.

It is very important for us to practice all these good habits, not only in this special month but we must train ourselves to also include all of these good things in our daily life too. Ramadaan comes as a reminder to us to show us that if we can do all of these beautiful deeds in this month then we can surely continue all of what we have learnt so far for the rest of the year.

We can do this!

You can do this!

The end

Ramadaan Mubaarak!

[Have a blessed Ramadaan]

Acknowledgements

I would like to thank my mother who has always been an inspiration to me, for believing in me and supporting me. Thank you, mom!

A special thank you to my husband for the endless support.

I would also like to thank one of our dear friends, Mr. R.T. Richards, who has given me valuable insight and feedback on this lovely book.

About the Author

Sakina is a half Moroccan half Dutch mother of three who is passionate about creating stories that inspire and delight young readers. With a background in childhood education, parenting and storytelling, she enjoys crafting books that spark imagination and education to foster a love for reading. As a parent and former teaching assistant Sakina understands the joy of sharing meaningful stories with children. When not writing Sakina enjoys spending time with her family, being in nature or reading with her children.

www.ingramcontent.com/pod-product-compliance
Lightning Source LLC
Chambersburg PA
CBHW040815120626

46547CB00005B/552